ISBN 0 947338 57 8

This edition published 1994 exclusively for Selecta Book Ltd,
Folly Road, Roundway, Devizes, Wiltshire, UK.

FAITH ENDURING

Original Illuminated texts
from the P.F. Sunman
Nostalgia Collection

Photographs by
Graham McGeagh

If you awake and see the
sunrise
Bathing earth in red and
gold,
As you gaze you'll
somehow find
It fills one with anticipation
To start the day with such
a sight.
God is so very good to give
A fresh new day,
giftwrapped so bright.

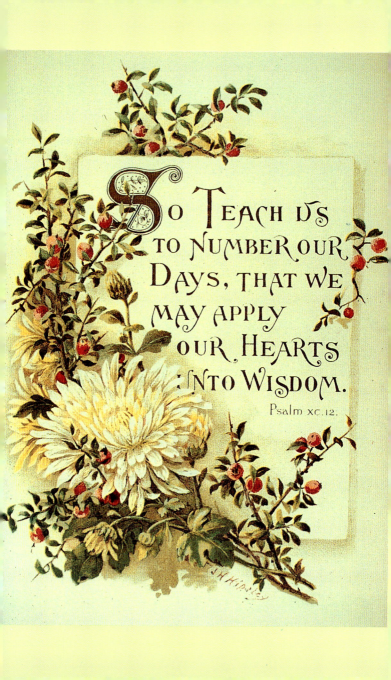

So Teach us to Number our Days, that we may apply our Hearts into Wisdom.

Psalm xc. 12.

O Divine Master, grant
that I may not so much
seek to be consoled as to
console;
To be understood as to
understand;
To be loved, as to love;
For it is in giving that we
receive,
It is in pardoning that we
are pardoned,
And it is in dying that we
are born to Eternal Life.

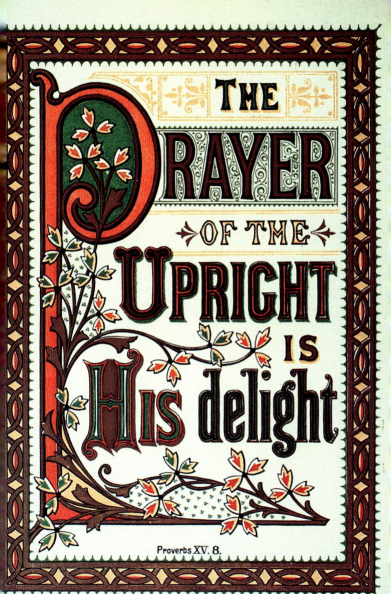

THE PRAYER OF THE UPRIGHT IS HIS delight

Proverbs XV. 8.

Kronheim & Co., London.

Faith makes
The uplook good
The outlook bright,
The inlook favourable,
And the future glorious.

THE LIGHT
THAT IS
FELT

A tender child of summers three,
  Seeking her little bed at night,
Paused on the dark stair timidly,
"Oh Mother! take my hand," said she
  "And then the dark will all be light."

We older children grope our way
  From dark behind to dark before;
And only when our hands we lay,
Dear Lord, in thine, the night is day,
  And there is darkness nevermore.

Reach downward to the sunless days,
  Wherein our guides are blind as we,
And faith is small, and hope delays;
Take thou the hands of prayer we raise,
  And let us feel the light of Thee.

Whittier

J.H.Hipsley

ALF COOKE LEEDS.

Let nothing disturb you,
let nothing frighten you
everything passes away
except God;
God alone is sufficient.

St Theresa

THOU wilt keep him in perfect peace, whose mind is stayed on Thee because he TRUSTETH in Thee.

Isa. XXVI. 3.

Teach me, my God and King,
In all things Thee to see,
And what I do in anything
To do it as for Thee.

George Herbert 1593-1633

With bounty free

Of luscious fruit from bending vine

And laden tree

Doth Autumn mark the year's decline.

The sunflower shows her disc of flame,

The hedgerows yield their hardy spoil,

And fields of waving corn proclaim

A blessing on man's daily toil.

S. E. G.

Blessed is the person who has
learned to admire but not
to envy,
to follow but not to imitate,
to praise but not to flatter,
and to learn but
not manipulate.

BLESSED·ARE·THE·PURE
IN·HEART : FOR · THEY
SHALL · SEE · GOD.

True peace is not an uneasy truce; it is the fruit of genuine openness and forgiveness.

Oh that I were an Orange Tree
That busy plant!
Then should I ever laden be
And never want
Some fruit for Him that dresseth me.

George Herbert

THE FRUIT OF THE SPIRIT IS LOVE,
JOY, PEACE, LONGSUFFERING
GENTLENESS, GOODNESS, FAITH
MEEKNESS, TEMPERANCE:

Galatians
V. 22

O Lord, Thou knowest how
busy I must be this day;
If I forget Thee, do not
Thou forget me.
Sir Jacob Astley

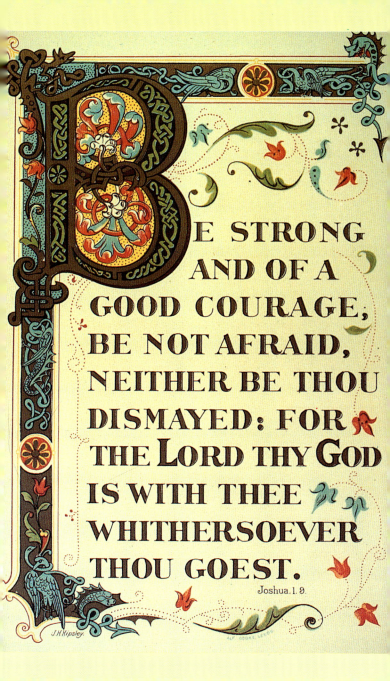

BE STRONG AND OF A GOOD COURAGE, BE NOT AFRAID, NEITHER BE THOU DISMAYED: FOR THE LORD THY GOD IS WITH THEE WHITHERSOEVER THOU GOEST.

Joshua. 1. 9.

J.H.Hipsley.

ALF COOKE, LEEDS.

This above all - to thine own
self be true,
And it must follow, as the
night the day,
Thou canst not be false
to any man.

William Shakespeare
from Hamlet

As sunlight pierces the
    mountain mists,
And lightens the
    valleys below.
So may the sun of
    life, arise
And scatter the clouds
    with its glow.

I wish thee the day's
    full strength and joy,
And the golden
    sunset light;
To brighten the evening
    of life, before
The fall of the
    peaceful night.

If you read history, you
will find that Christians
who did the most for the
present world, were those
who thought the most
of the next.

C S Lewis

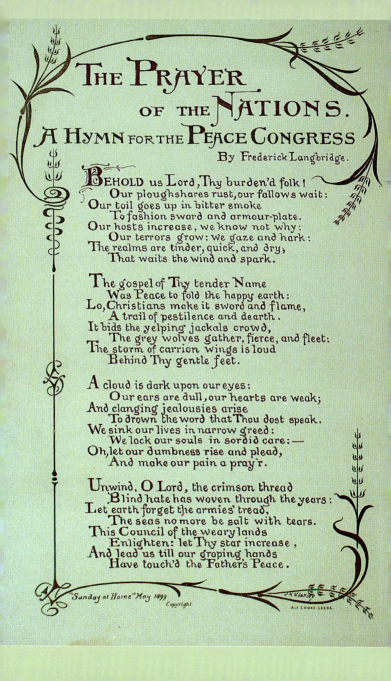

THE PRAYER
OF THE NATIONS.
A HYMN FOR THE PEACE CONGRESS

By Frederick Langbridge.

BEHOLD us Lord, Thy burden'd folk!
 Our ploughshares rust, our fallows wait:
Our toil goes up in bitter smoke
 To fashion sword and armour-plate.
Our hosts increase, we know not why:
 Our terrors grow: we gaze and hark:
The realms are tinder, quick, and dry,
 That waits the wind and spark.

The gospel of Thy tender Name
 Was Peace to fold the happy earth:
Lo, Christians make it sword and flame,
 A trail of pestilence and dearth.
It bids the yelping jackals crowd,
 The grey wolves gather, fierce, and fleet:
The storm of carrion wings is loud
 Behind Thy gentle feet.

A cloud is dark upon our eyes:
 Our ears are dull, our hearts are weak;
And clanging jealousies arise
 To drown the word that Thou dost speak.
We sink our lives in narrow greed:
 We lock our souls in sordid care:—
Oh, let our dumbness rise and plead,
 And make our pain a pray'r.

Unwind, O Lord, the crimson thread
 Blind hate has woven through the years:
Let earth forget the armies' tread,
 The seas no more be salt with tears.
This Council of the weary lands
 Enlighten: let Thy star increase,
And lead us till our groping hands
 Have touch'd the Father's Peace.

Keep praying, but be thankful that God's answers are wiser than your prayers.

Since not alone
In praise of brighter hours
they sing,
Whose hearts have known
The good adversity can bring,

Stern Winter, let us weave thy
crown
Of hardy leaves and berries
blent;
We see the smile behind thy
frown,
And welcome thee in wisdom
sent.

S. E. G.

I thought I heard the
voice of God,
And climbed the
highest steeple.
But God declared,
'Go down again,
I dwell among the people.'

As a watchman waits for day,
And looks for light, and looks again;
When the night grows cold and gray
To be relieved he calls amain:
    So look, so wait,
    So long mine eyes
    To see my Lord
    My Sun, arise.

PHINEAS FLETCHER.

Let us with a gladsome mind Praise
the Lord for
he is kind,
For his mercies ay endure,
Ever faithful ever sure.

John Milton 1608-1674

He healeth the broken
in Heart, and bindeth
up their Wounds.

He telleth the number
of the Stars:
He calleth them all
by their names.

Psalm, CXLVII, 3, 4.

J H Kipsley

The Bible is the one book to
which any thoughtful person
may go with any honest
question of life or destiny and
find the answer of
God by honest searching.

PEACE

My soul, there is a country
Afar beyond the stars,
Where stands a winged sentry
All skilful in the wars:

There above noise and danger,
Sweet Peace sits, crowned with smiles
And one borne in a manger
Commands the beauteous files.

He is thy Gracious Friend,
And (O my soul awake!)
Did in pure love descend,
To die here for thy sake.

If thou canst get but thither,
There grows the flower of peace,
The rose that cannot wither,
Thy fortress and thine ease,

Leave then thy foolish ranges;
For none can thee secure,
But one who never changes,
Thy God, thy Life, thy Cure.

Henry Vaughan

I believe in the sun even
when it is not shining.
I believe in love even
when I feel it not.
I believe in God even
when he seems to be silent.

MAY THE LORD HIMSELF
BE

YOUR

DEFENCE!

Although we are parted I never forget you
Often and often I think of you still
Praying our Father each year to be with you
Guiding, protecting and shielding from ill.

Charlotte Murray

There is a past which has
gone forever, but there is a
future which is still our own.

Trusting

Trusting in the morning
At the sun's first ray
For the strength to serve Christ
Through the coming day,

For the faith to follow
If my path be dim,
For the grace which makes me
More and more like Him

God give me work
Till my life shall end.
And life
Till my work is done.

Written on
Winifred Holtby's Grave

Sweet Spring, awake
The sunshine in our northern skies!
Bid Nature take
Once more for us her fairest guise.
So in thy promise we will read,
Foreshadowed by thy quick'ning breath,
Fulfilment of the wondrous creed
That life shall triumph over death.

S. E. G.

Duty makes us do things well, but love makes us do them beautifully.

Rev Phillip Brooks

WHATSOEVER·YE·DO·IN·WORD·OR·DEED

Teach me my God and King,
In all things Thee to see,
And what I do in any thing,
To do it as for Thee;

All may of Thee partake:
Nothing can be so mean,
Which with his tincture for thy sake
Will not grow bright and clean.

Not rudely as a beast,
To run into an action;
But still to make Thee prepossest
And give it his perfection.

A servant with this clause,
Makes drudgery divine:
Who sweeps a room, as for Thy laws
Makes that and the action fine

A man that looks on glass,
On it may stay his eye;
Or if he pleaseth, through it pass,
And then the heaven espy.

This is the famous stone
That turneth all to gold;
For that which God doth touch & own
Cannot for less be told.

George Herbert

DO·ALL·IN·THE·NAME·OF·THE·LORD·JESUS

Lord, make me an
instrument of your peace!
Where there is hatred let me
sow love;
Where there is injury,
pardon;
Where there is doubt,
faith;
Where there is despair,
hope;
Where there is darkness,
light;
Where there is sadness,
joy.

Prayer of
St Francis (attributed)

Lord, what wilt
Thou have
me to do?

Acts 9, 6.

*Do not pray by heart
but with heart.*

For the Lord God is a Sun and Shield: The Lord will give Grace and Glory: no Good Thing will He withhold from them that Walk Uprightly. Psalm LXXXIV 11

Jesus, Sun and Shield art Thou;
Sun and Shield for ever!
Never canst thou cease to shine,
Cease to guard us never.
Cheer our steps as on we go.
Come between us and the Foe.

Bonar

J. K. Ripsley

ALF COOKE LEEDS.

I have found the paradox
that if I love until it hurts,
then there is no hurt,
but only more love.

Mother Teresa

The God of peace.......
make you
perfect in every
good work to
do His will,

working in you
that which is wellpleasing
in His sight.

Heb. 13, 20. 21.

Faith is like love:
it cannot be forced.

Arthur Schopenhaver.
1788-1860

Ye ice falls! ye that from the mountains brow
Adown enormous ravines slope amain,
Torrents, methinks, that heard a mighty voice,
And stopped at once amid the maddest plunge!
Motionless torrents! silent cataracts!
Who made you glorious as the gates of Heaven
Beneath the keen full moon? Who made the sun
Clothe you with rainbows? Who with living flowers
Of loveliest blue, spread garlands at your feet?
God! let the torrents, like a shout of nations,
Answer! and let the ice plains echo, God!
God! sing ye meadow streams with gladsome voice!
Ye pine groves, with your soft and soullike sounds!
And they, too, have a voice, yon piles of snow,
And in their perilous fall shall thunder, God!

Rhone Glacier.

COLERIDGE.

A miracle is an event which
creates faith. Frauds deceive.
An event which creates faith
does not deceive;
therefore it is not a fraud,
but a miracle.

George Bernard Shaw

Glad Summer time,
The pledge of Heaven's sweet
favour near,
The golden prime
Of all the varied circling year.

Ah, surely when God's lavish hand
Doth freely scatter fruits
and flowers,
There cometh to the happy land
A dream of Eden's long
lost bowers.

S. E. G.

*Life without faith is an
arid business.*

Noel Coward

As many as are led by the Spirit of God they are the sons of GOD

Rom. 8.14

When life seems difficult
and the road ahead is steep,
Remember God didn't make
the earth flat, and it is more
interesting and beautiful
because of that.

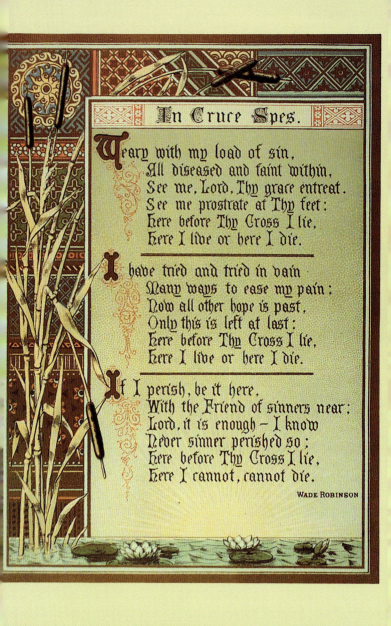

In Cruce Spes.

Weary with my load of sin,
All diseased and faint within,
See me, Lord, Thy grace entreat.
See me prostrate at Thy feet:
Here before Thy Cross I lie,
Here I live or here I die.

I have tried and tried in vain
Many ways to ease my pain:
Now all other hope is past,
Only this is left at last:
Here before Thy Cross I lie,
Here I live or here I die.

If I perish, be it here.
With the Friend of sinners near:
Lord, it is enough – I know
Never sinner perished so:
Here before Thy Cross I lie,
Here I cannot, cannot die.

WADE ROBINSON

God be in my head,
and in my understanding;
God be in my eyes,
and in my looking;
God be in my mouth,
and in my speaking;
God be in my heart,
and in my thinking;
God be at my end,
and at my departing.

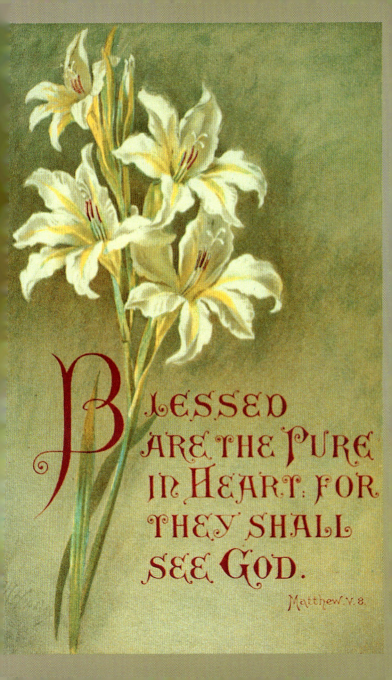

BLESSED ARE THE PURE IN HEART: FOR THEY SHALL SEE GOD.

Matthew. v. 8.

The more of doubt,
the stronger the faith,
I say,
if faith overcomes doubt.

Robert Browning

THE · FIRST · CHRISTMAS · CAROL

GLORIA · IN · EXCELSIS

The Country folk with eager eyes,
The stable door came flocking round;
And "Shepherds, there," they cried, "He lies
And there the Babe ye seek is found:
At Caesar's call, from south to north,
Our tribe is told in Bethlehem:
And priest and Levite thrust them forth, —
The ox's stall was meet for them."

The shepherds came—a simple crew,
In rustic order bent they there;
And still the shepherd pipes they blew,
And sang betimes a solemn air:
They bent, they gazed, "to God the praise:"
They rose, and hymn'd their hymn again;
It seem'd a strain of elder days,
When God vouchsafed to walk with men.

And then they told how late at night,
By David's Well they watch'd their fold;
The bale was wall'd to left and right,
And screen'd their huddling sheep from cold.
God's angel stoop'd in bright array,
"Fear not," he said. "but shout and sing;
To you, in David's town, this day
Is born a Saviour, Christ the King.

"And this shall be the sign: ye'll find
The Babe within a manger laid."
Then sudden o'er the angel shined
The heavenly host: on harps they play'd.
And, while he mounted in their light,
From sky to earth the chorus ran,
"Glory to God in highest height,
Peace upon earth, good-will to man."

Faith is putting all your eggs
in God's basket.
Then counting your blessings
before they hatch.

Romona C Carroll

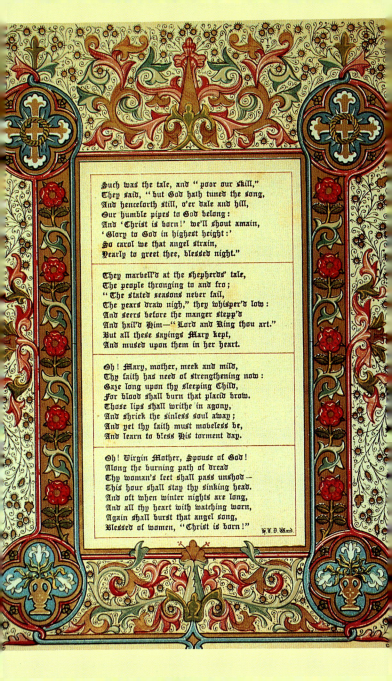

Such was the tale, and " poor our skill,"
They said, " but God hath tuned the song,
And henceforth still, o'er vale and hill,
Our humble pipes to God belong :
And 'Christ is born!' we'll shout amain,
'Glory to God in highest height :'
So carol we that angel strain,
Yearly to greet thee, blessed night."

They marvell'd at the shepherds' tale,
The people thronging to and fro ;
" The stated seasons never fail,
The years draw nigh," they whisper'd low :
And seers before the manger stepp'd
And hail'd Him—" Lord and King thou art."
But all these sayings Mary kept,
And mused upon them in her heart.

Oh ! Mary, mother, meek and mild,
Thy faith has need of strengthening now :
Gaze long upon thy sleeping Child,
For blood shall burn that placid brow.
Those lips shall writhe in agony,
And shriek the sinless soul away ;
And yet thy faith must moveless be,
And learn to bless His torment day.

Oh ! Virgin Mother, Spouse of God !
Along the burning path of dread
Thy woman's feet shall pass unshod —
This hour shall stay thy sinking head.
And oft when winter nights are long,
And all thy heart with watching worn,
Again shall burst that angel song,
Blessed of women, " Christ is born !"

W. J. D. Wmd.

Mercy is Love being
gracious.
Eloquence is Love talking.
Prophecy is Love foretelling.
Faith is Love believing.
Charity is Love acting.
Sacrifice is Love offering
itself.
Patience is Love waiting.
Endurance is Love abiding.
Hope is Love expecting.
Peace is Love resting.
Prayer is Love communing.

Psalm 23

The Lord is my shepherd,
I shall not be in want
He makes me lie down in
green pastures,
He leads me beside quiet waters,
He restores my soul.
He guides me in paths of
righteousness
for his name's sake.
Even though I walk through
the valley
of the shaddow of death
I will fear no evil,
for you are with me;
Your rod and your staff,
they comfort me.

Faith Enduring

Reproductions of illuminated texts
from old devotional books of the
Victorian era, featuring lavishly
embellished borders, calligraphic texts
and appealing drawings and
paintings are used to illustrate these
pages. With well known verses that
bring comfort and encouragement
from the Old and New Testaments,
with some prayers also being included.

Original embellished texts from the
P.F. Sunman Nostalgia
Collection.